Stickchic and Stickman's Guide to

The 8 date rule

For those of you who are sick of dating
Mr. or Ms. Not Quite Right

Written by Minnie King

Illustrated by Hristina Bashevski

When I started dating, my mother told me to stick to *The Eight Date Rule*. Of course, I didn't listen. After several (well, actually quite a few) years of unsuccessful relationships, it became evident that mum was right.

When you meet someone new and attractive, your better judgement is often temporarily impaired by the hormones coursing through your body. Common sense can depart at approximately the same time. If you are dating for a good time, not a long time, these feelings can be a lot of fun.

However, if you're looking for a relationship that has the potential to last, it may be time to temporarily place your hormones on hold and keep a clear head. This is required because a relationship based on anything other than genuine affection and mutual respect will eventually fail. Remember, if you are looking for a long-term partner, you are looking for someone who has the potential to become your best friend. Therefore, the earlier you can decide whether or not you like each other's character, the better. Don't let racing hormones confuse you. The person you choose as your long-term partner will irrevocably change your life for the better or worse. So, it is wise to take your time and make a good decision.

In order to achieve the clarity of mind required for unclouded decision-making, **for eight dates there should be no physical contact**. You simply hang out as friends. This gives you the time and space to discover who the other person *really* is, and whether or not you want to continue spending your valuable time together. If you decide you are not suited, you can both move on with your lives with no harm done.

"If you always do what you've always done, you'll always get what you've always got."

Henry Ford.

Stickchic was single. She was happy but was starting to wonder if her mother was right.

She just couldn't seem to find Mr. Right.

Then, one day, she had an idea.

She consulted her friends and made a list of her perfect man's attributes.

Then she went looking for him. She tried door knocking.

The supermarket.

Masquerading as an air hostess at the airport.

She frequented the hospital.

And enlisted the help of the Emergency Services.

But all to no avail. Mr. Right was nowhere to be found.

Stickman was single too. He had tried all his best lines, but even when they worked, he never met Ms. Right, only Ms. Not-Quite-Right.

Stickman was determined to find the woman of his dreams.

He made a list of what he was looking for in his perfect lady.

Then, he began his search. First, he tried yoga.

Then ballet.

He expanded his search by joining the local women's basketball team.

And leading the cheer squad at the ladies football club.

He joined a knitting circle

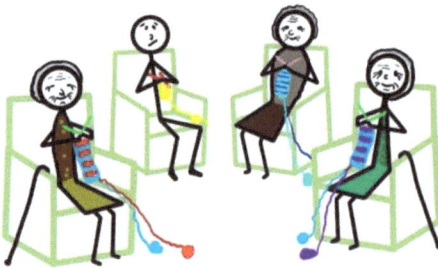

And made some great friends but Ms. Right was as elusive as ever.

He started to wonder if he would ever find her.

He phoned his mum for some helpful advice.

Then one day they met.

They both decided that this time things would be different. They would learn from their previous mistakes and use *The Eight Date Rule.*

FIRST DATE: THE MOVIES

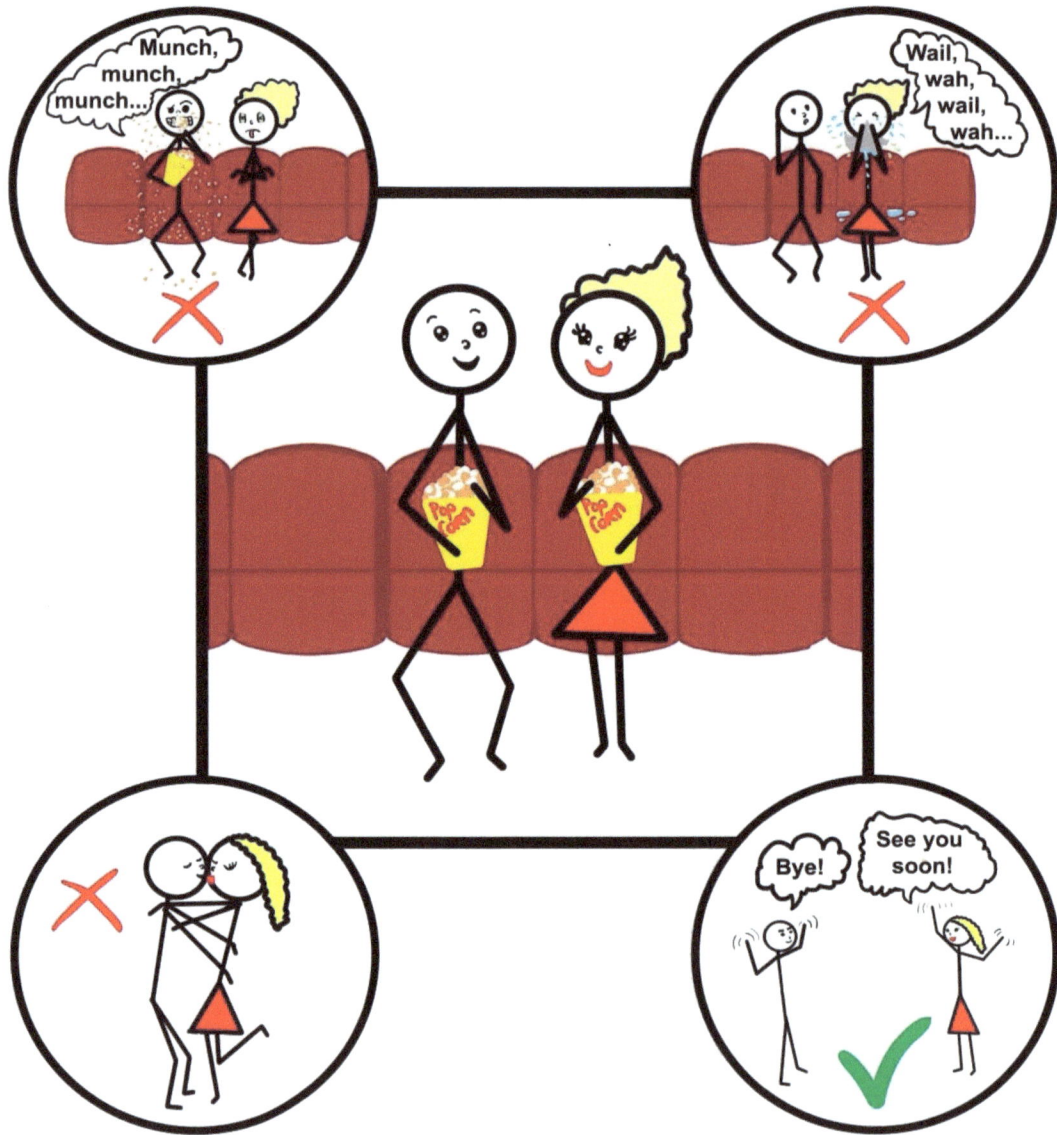

SECOND DATE: THE BOWLING ALLEY

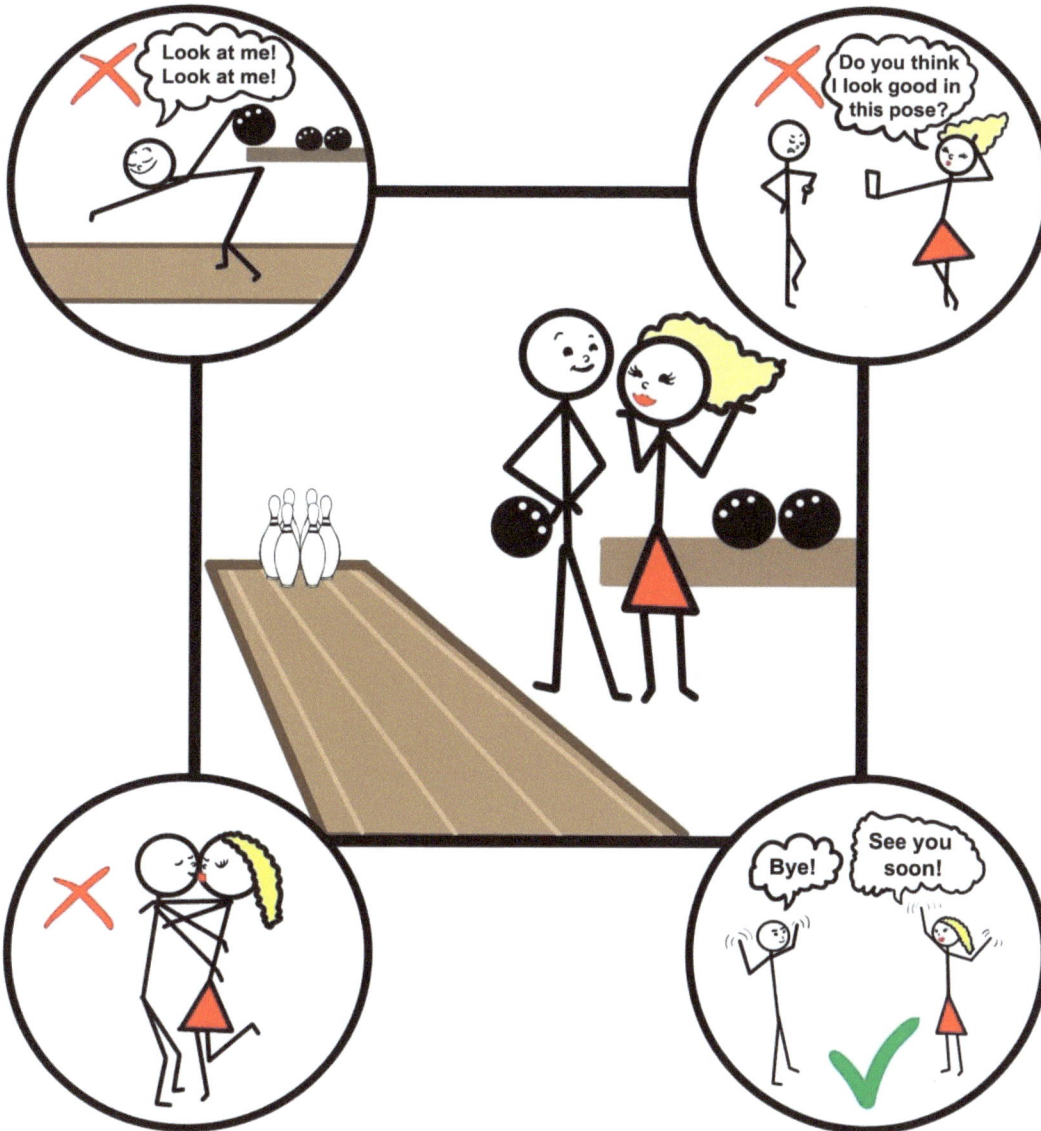

THIRD DATE: A QUIET RESTAURANT

FOURTH DATE: A NATURE HIKE

FIFTH DATE: A COUNTRY DRIVE

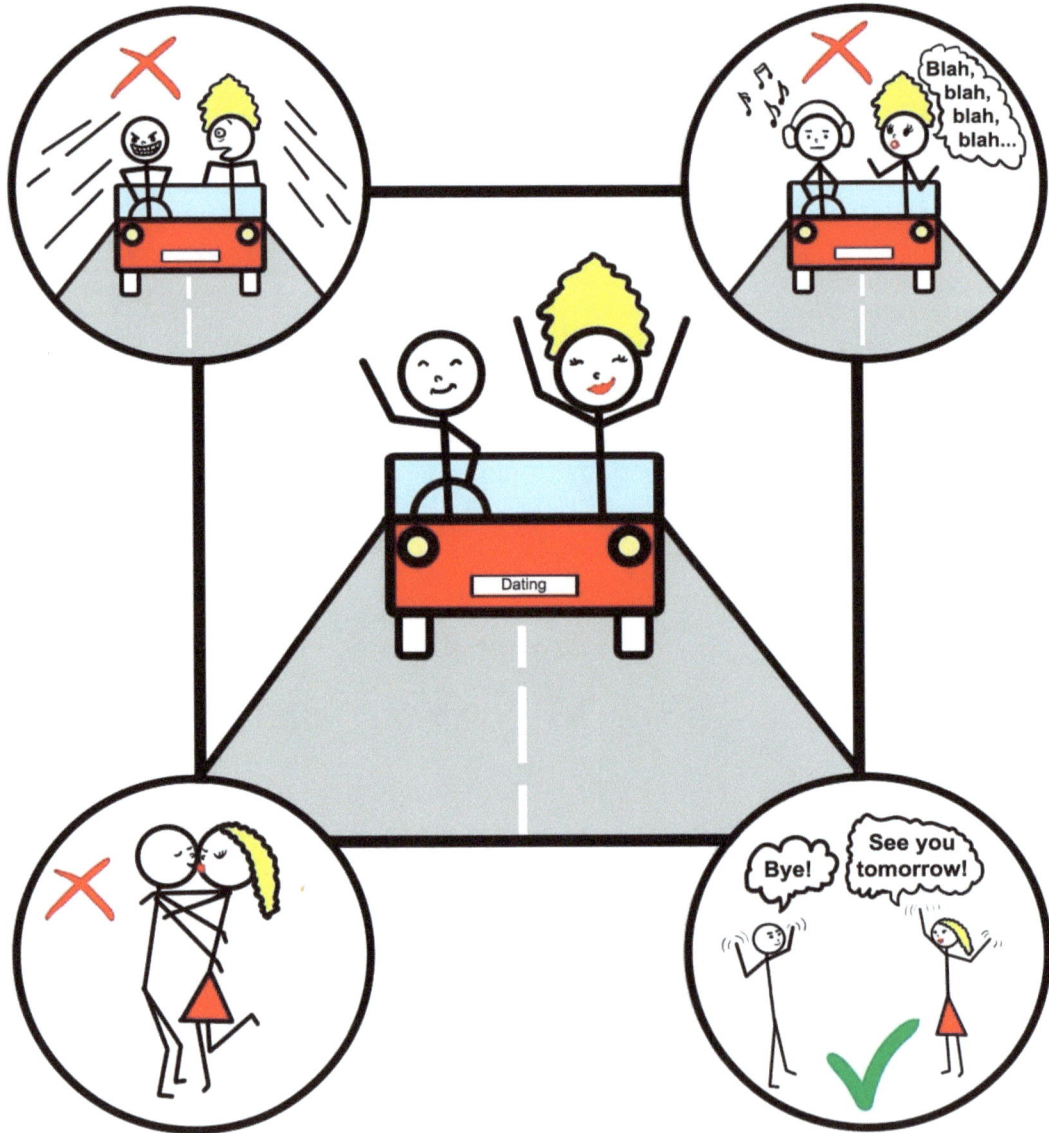

SIXTH DATE: A RELAXING BIKE RIDE

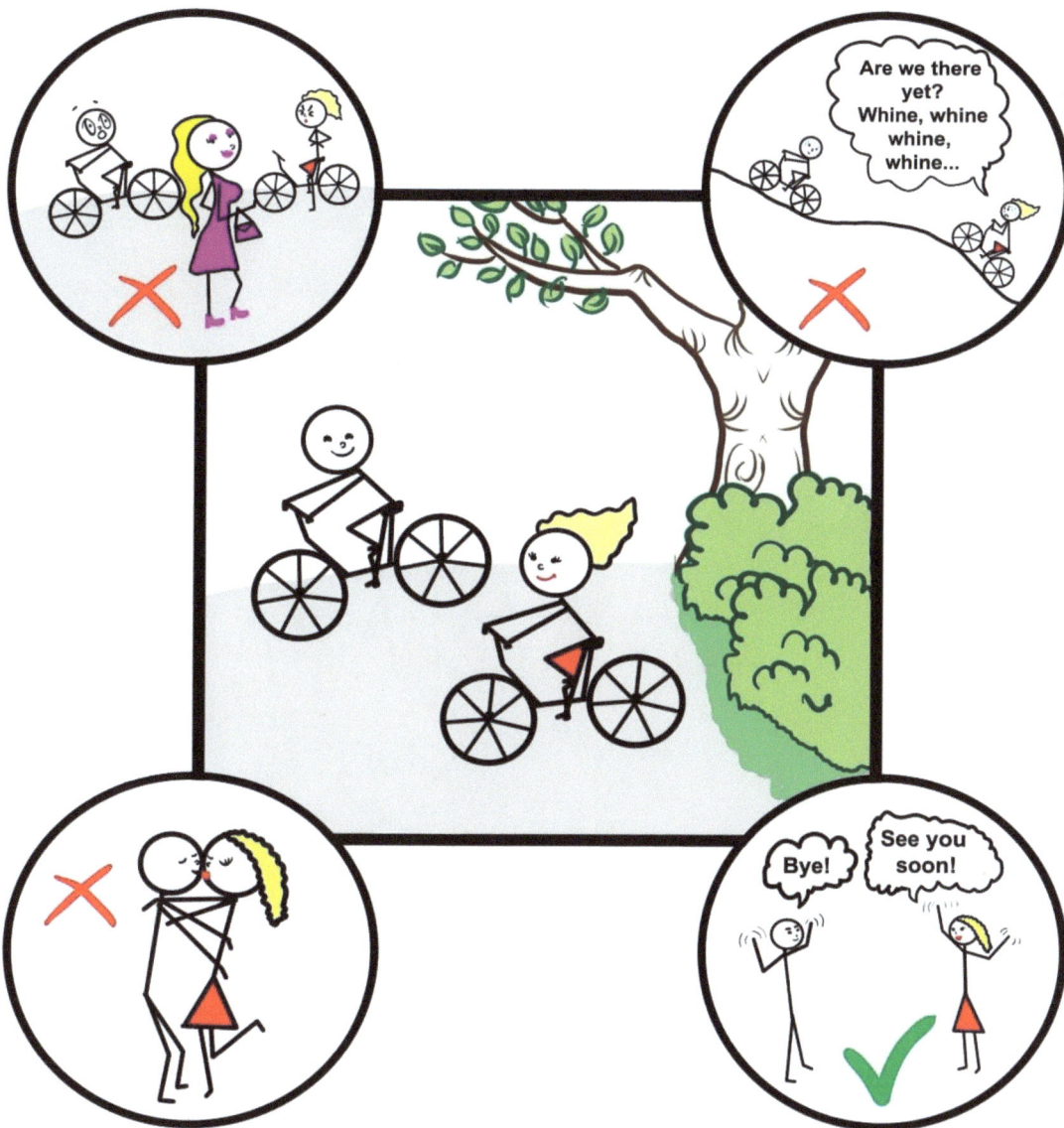

SEVENTH DATE: MEETING THE FRIENDS

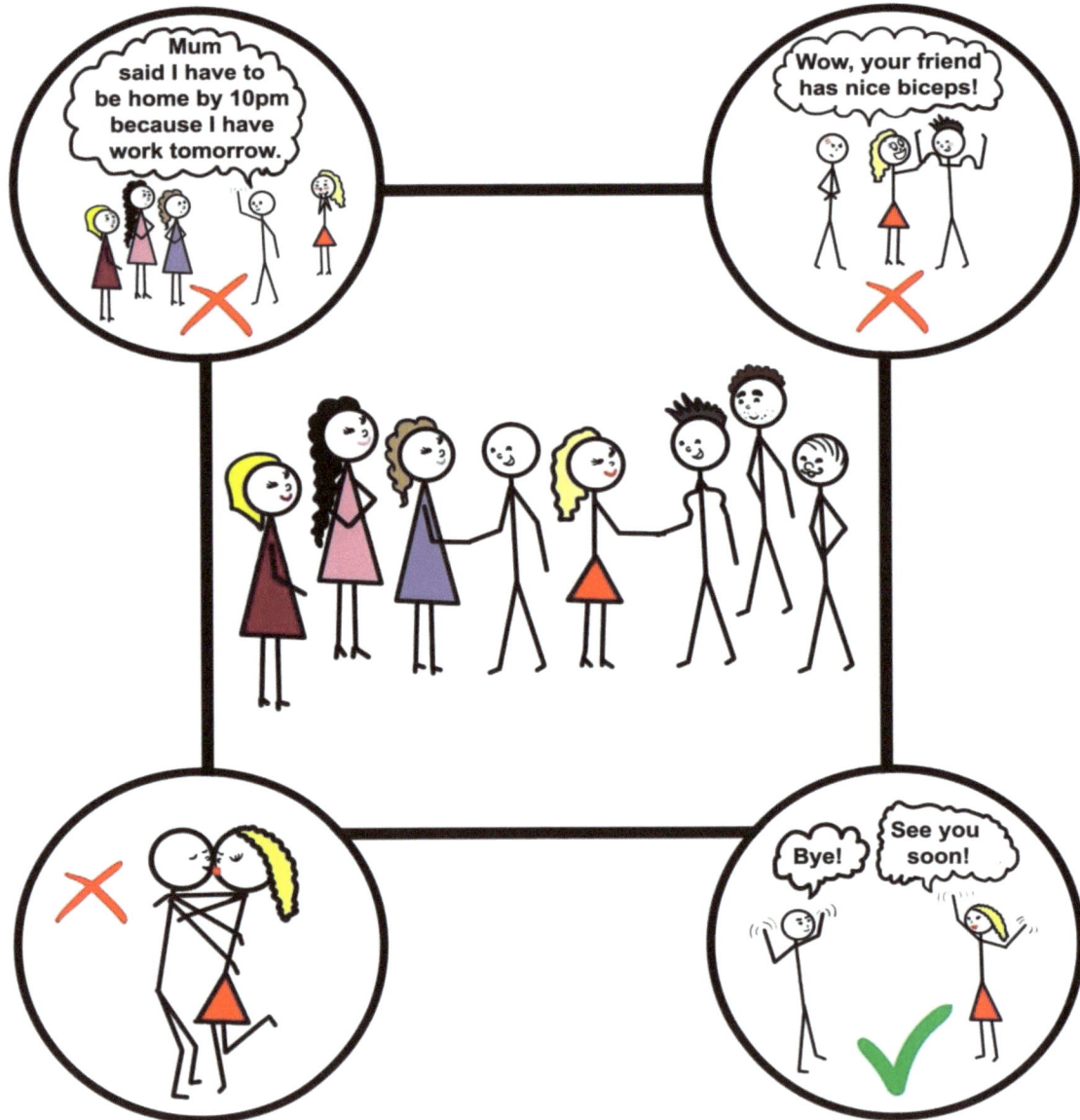

EIGHTH DATE: ROMANTIC DINNER AT HOME

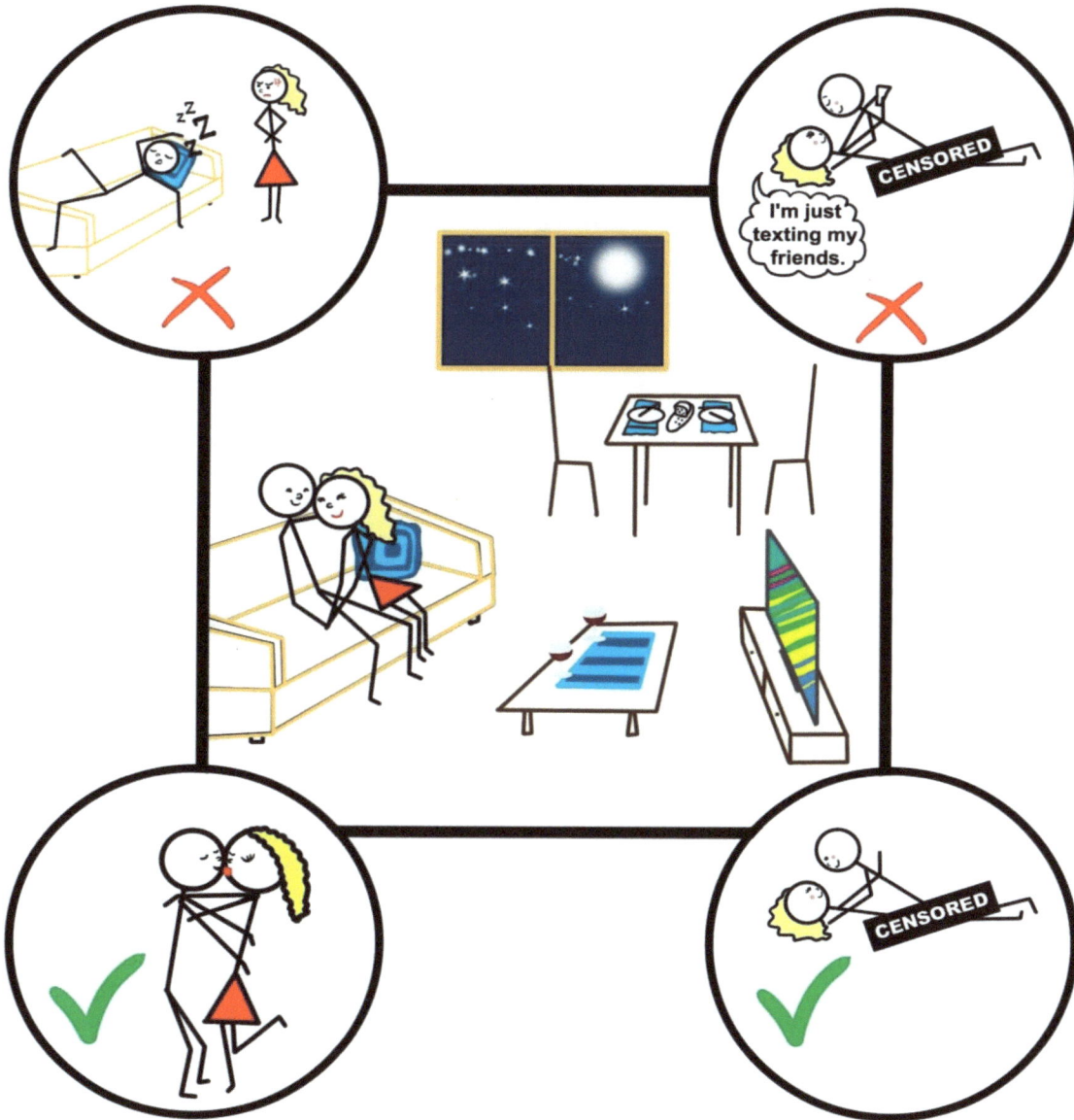

After eight dates, they knew they could be BFF's (Best Friends Forever).

And so, they lived happily ever after. Well, almost.....

For Carl

Other Books You Might Enjoy

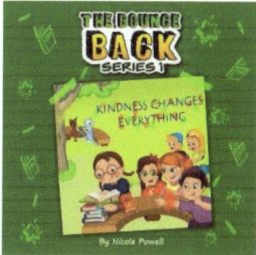

Kindness Changes Everything is the first book in *The Bounce Back Series*. It addresses the serious issue of schoolyard bullying from the perspective of both the victim and the perpetrator. It equips children with the strategies they need to overcome adversity and be resilient when facing such challenges. This provides the most valuable rewards of all: self-respect, respect for others and the opportunity to live a life they can love.

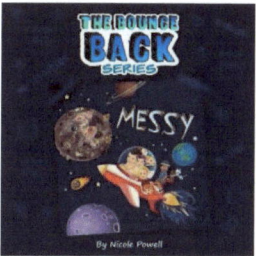

Messy is the second book in *The Bounce Back Series*. It encourages children to develop a healthy respect for themselves, each other and the Earth that underpins all life. *Messy* develops the understanding that actions have consequences and that mistakes are simply learning opportunities. It encourages children to treat themselves and each other with gentleness, kindness and forgiveness. These are invaluable skills in an increasingly demanding world.

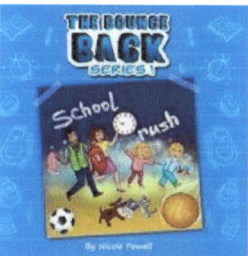

School Rush is the third book in *The Bounce Back Series*. It is designed to help children begin working with their emotions in a positive and healthy way. Instead of school mornings being filled with chaos, frustration and tension, they can be transformed into a time of warmth, fun and laughter, as family members help each other to leave the house on time.

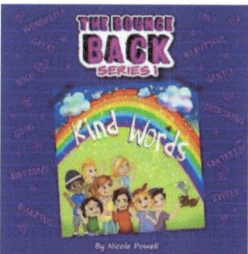

Kind Words is the fourth book in *The Bounce Back Series*. It is designed to help children address everyday school yard difficulties by equipping them with sound conflict resolution strategies. When children learn to work with their emotions in a positive and healthy way they can more readily understand differing perspectives and resolve conflicts in a happy and mutually beneficial manner. As a result, they can enjoy an improved relationship with themselves and others, and are more able to develop supportive, enduring friendships that can last a lifetime.

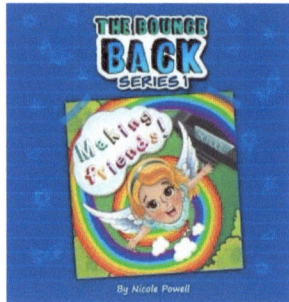

Making Friends is the fifth book in *The Bounce Back Series*. It equips children with strategies they can use, should they find themselves alone in the schoolyard at play. The majority of children will experience this at some point in their school lives. This type of social isolation can be extremely distressing for a child (and their parents!) *Making Friends* encourages children to see themselves as the creators of their own destiny rather than victims. Once they understand this, they can extrapolate it to the rest of their lives and enjoy a greater sense of confidence and ease in their surroundings.

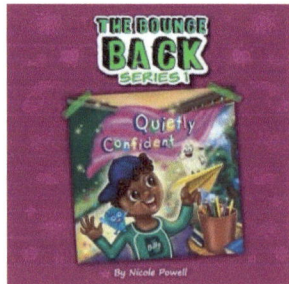

Quietly Confident is the sixth book in *The Bounce Back Series*. It addresses the emotion of fear which unconsciously underpins many of our choices in life. By encouraging children to understand and face this emotion directly, they can enjoy an increased sense of confidence, freedom, and empowerment.

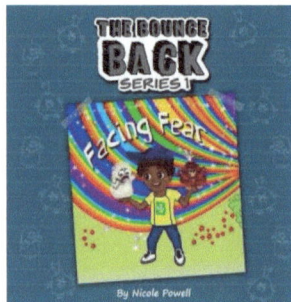

Facing Fear is the seventh book in *The Bounce Back Series*. It follows on from *Quietly Confident* and continues to address the emotion of fear. It explains that anger is often used to mask other emotions that are more difficult for us to feel, such as fear, shame or guilt. When children learn to accept and understand the underlying causes of anger, it has no need to arise. As a result, children can enjoy an increased sense of calm, happiness and peace within themselves. Thus, improving their relationships with the people who surround them.

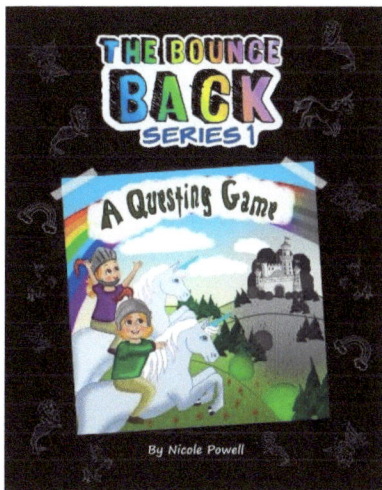

A Questing Game engages children's imaginations as they embark on an adventure that can only begin when they are tucked up in bed at night or calmly resting.

The game encourages children to relax, develops their imagination and cultivates desirable personality traits such as kindness, helpfulness, generosity and compassion. It also encourages a positive internal dialogue which enhances self-esteem.

If you have trouble getting your children into bed at night then this game is for you!

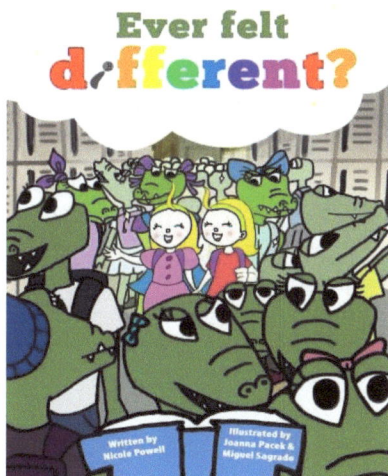

Ever Felt Different? is for anyone who has ever felt different.

Two little girls, delivered to the wrong families at birth by a disorientated stork, have nothing in common with the other children in their neighbourhood.

They don't look the same, behave the same, or like any of the same things.

Although the girls are teased and left out by some of the other children, their mother's love and encouragement helps them to believe in themselves and follow their dreams. They learn to like and accept themselves just as they are and realise that their uniqueness is one of their greatest strengths. In fact, it is only *because* they are different that they soar to great heights.

Cover Illustration Copyright © 2017 by Nattyboo
Cover design by Minnie King and Hristina Bashevski
Editing by Kerry Thornton (Chief Editor), John Clancy and Andrew McCallum from Upwork.

First Printing, 2017

ISBN **978-0-6481471-1-4**

Nattyboo Publishing
PO Box 177
GRANGE, SA, 5022

www.nattyboo.com

www.ingramcontent.com/pod-product-compliance
Lightning Source LLC
Chambersburg PA
CBHW041240040426

42445CB00004B/97